YE OLDE

CAT MEMES

YE OLDE

CAT MEMES

THE ORIGINAL BOOK
of CAT HUMOR

By Eulalie Osgood Grover

COPYRIGHT 1911

PICTURES COPYRIGHTED *by* THE ROTOGRAPH CO.

HOUGHTON MIFFLIN HARCOURT
Boston • New York 2019

hmhbooks.com

Library of Congress Cataloging-in-Publication Data
Names: Grover, Eulalie Osgood, 1873–1958, author.
Title: Ye olde cat memes : the original book of cat humor /
by Eulalie Osgood Grover. Other titles: Kittens and cats
Description: Boston : Houghton Mifflin Harcourt, 2019. | "Originally
published in different form by Houghton Mifflin Company in 1911
under the title Kittens and Cats: A First Reader"—Verso title page.
Identifiers: LCCN 2019024063 (print) | LCCN 2019024064 (ebook) |
ISBN 9780358238416 (hardback) | ISBN 9780358246299 (ebook)
Subjects: LCSH: Readers (Primary) | Children's poetry. | Cats—
Humor—Juvenile literature. Classification: LCC PE1127.A6 G76 2019
(print) | LCC PE1127.A6 (ebook) | DDC 428.6—dc23
LC record available at https://lccn.loc.gov/2019024063
LC ebook record available at https://lccn.loc.gov/2019024064

Book design by RAPHAEL GERONI

Victorian Ornaments © Webalys / Shutterstock

Printed in the United States of America

WOZ 10 9 8 7 6 5 4 3 2 1

CONTENTS

I AM THE QUEEN

THE QUEEN

I am the Queen of all the Kittens.
I am the Queen! the Queen!
Come, all kittens and cats.
Hear what I have to say.
Tomorrow I give a grand party.
The party will be in my palace.
You are all invited!
From the biggest to the littlest,
from the oldest to the youngest.
So wash your paws and shine
your fur.
Forget your naughty tricks
and do not one of you dare be late
to your Queen's party.
To-morrow at one o'clock.

GRANNY GRAY

I am Granny Gray.
I am very, very old,
but I am still going to the Queen's
party.
I am grandmother to a great many
kittens.
When they are naughty,
their mothers always send for me.
When they are sick,
I always know what to do.
I teach them how to meow.
I teach them how to scratch.
I teach them how to catch mice.
I am very, very old.
They call me Granny Gray.

I AM GRANNY GRAY

GETTING READY

Hark, hark! What is that noise?
No, I cannot play with you now.
I must take my bath.
I must get ready for the party.
I have a new jacket and a new hat
to wear.

My pants were new last week, but
now they are not new.

I tore two holes in them when I
climbed the apple tree in the back
yard.

Mother patched them, but
somehow the patches show up more
than the holes did.

Perhaps my new jacket will cover
the patches.

I hope I shall look well dressed.

I AM TAKING MY BATH

I WONDER

I wonder if those horrid patches
    Upon my trousers light
Would show as much if they were not
    As dark as dark as night?

READY FOR THE PARTY

Mew! Mew! Mew! Mew!

Hurry, Mother, hurry!

We are all ready and waiting to start.

Yes, we are all here.

There are one, two, three, four of us.

The carriage is pretty small, but we think we can all get in.

We will be good this time and not push each other out.

But please do hurry, Mother.

It is hard to sit so still.

Mew! Mew! Mew! Mew!

WE ARE ALL HERE

A FULL CART

We are three little cats in a cart
   And one underneath on the floor,
The cart is so full we hardly see how
   There'll be any room for more.

I HAVE A NEW BONNET

HURRIED MOTHER

Dear me! My kittens are in such a hurry!

They give me no time to dress.

It takes a very long time to shine my fur and to fix my bonnet.

It is a new bonnet.

This is the first time I have worn it.

I hope it looks all right.

I must practice sitting up straight and proper just for a minute.

I want the Queen to know that I am a fine lady.

I hope my kittens will not rough up their fur.

If they do I shall have to groom them all over again.

Now we may start.

Where is their father?

PROUD FATHER

Here I am. Yes, I am the father of those four fine kittens.

They are such beautiful kittens, their mother does not even need to tie ribbons around their necks.

I am glad of that, for I do not like ribbons.

I must go now and take them all to the Queen's palace. I am sure they will be the handsomest kittens there.

I suppose I shall have to push their carriage.

Come, Mother, let us be off.
Are my whiskers stiff?
Is my hat on straight?

WAITING FOR THE CHILDREN

HIDING

Don't tell anybody where I am.

I am hiding away from Mother.

She wants me to go to the Queen's party and I don't want to go.

I don't like the Queen; she is so grand and dignified.

She frightens me.

I would rather hide in this pitcher all day than go to the Queen's palace.

Please don't tell where I am.

You will not, will you?

DON'T TELL ANYBODY

AN INVITATION

I've had an invitation
    To go to see the Queen,
But I'm a bashful kitten
    And I'd rather not be seen.

I HAVE A SICK HEAD

NO PARTY FOR ME

How strange it is
That some of us *want* to go to the party,
And some *do not* want to go.
Some of us *can* go,
And some *cannot* go.

I am one who *wants* to go,
And I am one who *cannot* go.

I have a sick head. It aches.
Perhaps I caught too many mice last night.

The doctor has been here.
He told me to take this medicine every
half-hour.

How I wish I could go to the party!

They surely will have something good
to eat there,
But I must stay at home and take my
medicine.

I'M OFF

I'm off for the Queen's palace.

I'm the only cat in our country who has an automobile.

But I suppose all the fine cats will be having them soon.

It is really great fun to ride faster than any cat or kitten can run.

I would invite you to ride too, but there is room for only one.

So, goodbye!

I'm off for the Queen's party.

IN MY AUTOMOBILE

HOW MUCH DO I WEIGH?

BEING WEIGHED

Yes, I am being weighed.

It frightens me to hang in the air like this.

What if I should fall, with my feet tied up in this bag!

I am sure I should be killed!

Can you see how much I weigh?

Nearly two pounds?

You don't mean it!

Then I am big enough to go to the party all alone,

Though I am not sure that I want to go.

I think I would rather stay at home and play.

THE PARTY

Attention, kittens and cats!
The clock strikes one.
The Queen's party has begun.

I am the Commanding Officer of the Palace. Attention to what I have to say!

Our Queen bids you welcome.
She waits for you in her throne room.

As you each pass in you must salute her and recite for her a cat tale, a rat tale, or some other tale, long or short, true or not.

But no fears or tears, for our Queen has a fine dinner in her grand dining room for all brave kittens and cats.

Now, who has the best tale?

I'VE A FEATHER IN MY CAP

THE COMMANDING OFFICER

I'm an officer of the Queen.
  I'm as proud can be,
For I've a feather in my cap,
  As anyone can see.

THE LATEST NEWS

We are here to bring great news,
O Queen!

We are here to bring great news!
Do you know—!
Do you know—!

Do you know a balloon
Has gone up to the moon!
The moon has been found
By a great, big balloon.
Up in a balloon,
Sailing round the moon.

Just think of that!
Hurrah for the balloon!
Hurrah for the big moon!

BREAKING THE NEWS

BREAKING THE NEWS

WHAT IS IT?

What's the news of the day,
Good neighbor, I pray?

They say a balloon
Has gone up to the moon.

THE SWEET SINGER

I'LL SING YOU A SONG

I am a famous singer among kittens and cats.

I sing in the kitten choir and in big concerts.

I wear a French bonnet when I sing.

My voice is very soft and very sweet.

I have come here today to sing for my Queen.

Purr-r, purr-r, purr-r!
I'll sing *you* a song,
Though not very long,
Yet I think it is as pretty as any.
Put your hand in your purse.
You'll never be worse,
And give the sweet singer a penny.

A TALE OF A MOUSE

Listen, O Queen, to this tale of a mouse!
"Hickory, dickory, dock,
The mouse ran up the clock;
The clock struck one,
And down he run,
Hickory, dickory, dock."

And we gobbled him up.

So, dear Queen, no mouse shall trouble your party while we two brave cats are here.

TWO BRAVE CATS

WE ARE THE CATS

Oh! We are the cats that caught the mouse,
That ran up the clock so fast.
The clock struck one, and down he run,
And we gobbled him up at last.

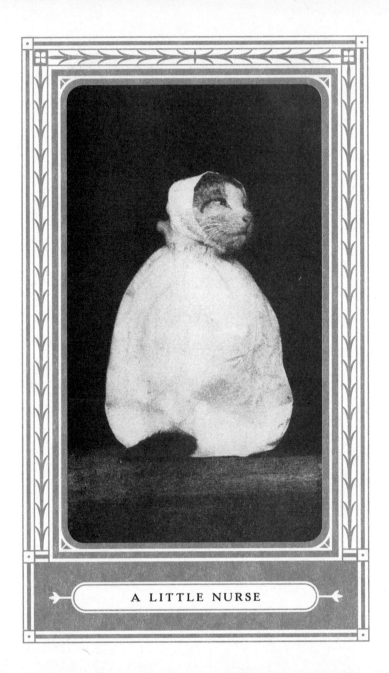

A LITTLE NURSE

THE NURSE'S TALE

I'm the nurse who takes care of kittens and cats when they are sick.

Sometimes they eat too much and have the stomachache.

Sometimes they fall down stairs and bump their heads.

Sometimes they get their tails bitten by bad dogs.

Then their mothers send for me and I take care of them until they are well.

I always wear a white dress and a white bonnet.

If you ever get sick, just send for me and I will take care of you.

A FAMOUS MOUSER

I am a famous mouser.
I have caught more mice than any other cat.

I can see them afar off.
I can hear them afar off.
I can scent them afar off.

They are all afraid of me.

They scurry away whenever they see me coming.

I wear soft pads on the bottom of my feet so they cannot hear me.

I keep my teeth white and sharp.
My friends call me the Mouse Trap.

But I know a kitty who is not a good mouser.
I will tell you about her.

THE MOUSE TRAP

This is my story:

Once there was a little Kitty,
　　White as the snow;
In the barn she used to frolic,
　　Long time ago.

In the barn a little Mousie
　　Ran to and fro;
For she heard the Kitty coming,
　　Long time ago.

Nine pearl teeth had little Kitty,
　　All in a row;
And they bit the little Mousie,
　　Long time ago.

When the teeth bit little Mousie,
　　Mousie cried, Oh!
But she got away from Kitty,
　　Long time ago.

No mouse ever slipped through my
　　Paws like that, I am glad to say.
I am a great mouser.
　　Yes, I am a famous mouser,
O Queen!

A DUNCE'S TALE

The other day in school I couldn't do my sums.

I couldn't tell how many two and two make.

I couldn't read my lesson.

I couldn't say my ABCs.

I couldn't sing my song.

So the teacher made me stand on a stool.

Then she put this cap on my head.

I have had to wear it ever since.

After this I am going to study hard.
I don't like to be called a dunce.
I don't like to sit on a stool.
Would you?

YES, I AM A DUNCE

THE KITTENS THAT LOST THEIR MITTENS

A TALE OF THREE KITTENS

We will tell you a tale of ourselves, dear Queen. A tale of three little kittens.

Three little kittens lost their mittens,
    And they began to cry,
    "O Mother dear,
    We very much fear
    That we have lost our mittens."

"Lost your mittens!
You naughty kittens!
Then you shall have no pie."
"Mee-ow, mee-ow, mee-ow!"
"No, you shall have no pie."
"Mee-ow, mee-ow, mee-ow!"

The three little kittens found their
mittens,
And they began to cry,
"O Mother dear,
See here, see here,
See! We have found our mittens."

"Put on your mittens,
You silly kittens,
And you may have some pie."

"Purr-r, purr-r, purr-r,
Oh, let us have the pie!
Purr-r, purr-r, purr-r."

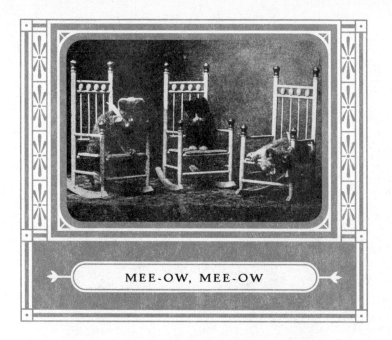

MEE-OW, MEE-OW

THE KITTENS THREE

Did you ever see the kittens three
That lost their mittens so red?
They hopped in chairs and looked about,
And meow and meow, they said.

HIS FATHER'S TROUSERS

A RAINY-DAY TALE

One day it rained and we could not go out of doors.

So my brothers and sisters and I played hide-and-seek in the attic.

All of a sudden one of my brothers said, "I'll tell you what let's do!"

"What's that?" we all asked together.

"Let's dress up! It's lots of fun."

So we ran to the closet where Father and Mother keep their Sunday clothes.

I put on Father's trousers, and now I wear them every day.

My brothers and sisters laugh at me. But I think I look fine—don't you?

A TALE OF
LONDON TOWN

If you should say:
   "Pussy-cat, pussy-cat,
Where have you been?"
   I should say:
"I've been to London
   To look at the Queen."
If you should say:
   "Pussy-cat, pussy-cat,
What did you there?"
   Then I should say:
"I frightened a little mouse
   From under her chair."
And she gave me these fine clothes.

THE HERO

HEY! DIDDLE, DIDDLE

A TALE I KNOW

Hey! diddle, diddle,
The cat and the fiddle.
The cow jumped over the moon;
The little dog laughed
To see such sport,
While the dish ran away with the
spoon.

I *know*, for *I* was the cat with the
fiddle.
I saw the cow jump over the moon.
I heard the little dog laugh.
I saw the dish run away with the
spoon.
Poor spoon!
I saw the whole of the fun.

Hey! diddle, diddle,
The cat and the fiddle!

A TALE OF ST. IVES

Listen, O Queen, to my wonderful tale.

As I was going to St. Ives,
I met a man with seven wives—
Every wife had seven sacks,
Every sack had seven cats,
Every cat had seven kits:
Kits, cats, sacks, and wives,
How many were there going to
St. Ives?

I have thought and counted, and
counted and thought, but I cannot
tell
how many were going to St. Ives.
Can you help me, wise Queen?

ON THE WAY TO ST. IVES

THEY CALL ME LITTLE FAIRY

A LITTLE FAIRY'S TALE

I am called Little Fairy.

Would you know that I am only a kitten, dear Queen?

Even the mice do not know it, for they play with me and we have fine frolics together.

One day a little mouse told me just where to find his house.

If he had known that I was a real live kitten, I am sure he never would have told me.

Would you like to know where the little mouse lives? A friend was with me and she will tell you.

Listen!

A SECRET

Yes, listen to my wonderful secret!
I asked the mouse,
"Where is your house?"
The mouse then said to me,
"Tell not the cat
And I'll tell thee.
Up stairs and down stairs,
Then straight ahead;
To the right, to the left,
Then bend down your head;
For there is my house
With the door so small,
That even a mouse
Can't go in if he's tall."

I KNOW A SECRET

WHO IS HE?

I have a strange tale, O Queen.
The other day I found a round
glass.
An old man was looking into the
glass, so I looked in, and guess what I
saw.
I saw a cat looking straight at me.
His face was white just like mine.

His eyes had black spots in them
Just like mine,
And his whiskers were long
Just like mine.

When I said "Mew!" he said "Mew!"

When I moved my paw, he moved
his paw.
When I ran away, he ran away too,
So I never have found out who he is.

BEHIND THE LOOKING GLASS

A STRANGER

I've met the cat that lives behind
    The looking glass, you see.
He's very handsome, and he looks
    For all the world like me.

MY PUSSY'S IN THE WELL

A SAD TALE

My pretty pussy is drowned,
is drowned!
Ding, dong, bell!
Pussy's in the well.
Who put her there?
Little Tommy Bear.
Who pulled her out?
Great Johnny Stout.
What a naughty boy was that,
To drown the poor, poor pussy-cat,
Who never did him any harm,
But killed the mice in his father's
barn.
I am sad, so sad, dear Queen!

MY OWN TALE

Pussy-cat Mew jumped over a coal,
And in her best petticoat burnt a
great hole.
Poor Pussy's weeping; she'll have no
more milk
Until her best petticoat's mended
with silk.

Mew! Mew! Mew!
I am Pussy-cat Mew.

PUSSY-CAT MEW

THREE TALES

I am the cat that caught the rat
that ate the malt
that lay in the house that Jack built.

I am the dog that worried the cat,
that caught the rat
that ate the malt
that lay in the house that Jack built.

I am the kitten all forlorn
that scratched the dog
that worried the cat
that caught the rat
that ate the malt
that lay in the house that Jack built.

A SIGHT TO SEE

The cat and the dog and the kitten
    Were as brave as brave could be,
But when they came to visit the Queen
    Why, they were a sight to see!

MY COURAGE DID FAIL

A 'FRAID-CAT'S TALE

Once I was a 'fraid-cat, dear
Queen.

All the kittens and cats laughed at
me and sang this song about me.

C was a cat who ran after a rat,
But her courage did fail
When he seized on her tail.
Now, what do you think that cat
did do?
She jumped in a chair and cried,
"Mew! mew!"

I was the cat who ran after the
rat.
But my courage did fail
When he seized on my tail.
"Mew! mew!"

FROM THE
NORTH POLE

I came from the land of the snow,
Where the summer is all day and
the winter is all night.

We dress in fur coats up there.

It's cold, so cold one can hardly
wink.

But I am proud of my land, for the
North Pole is there.

The dogs have seen it. They tell us
so.

And what the dogs say is true,
you know.

ALL BUNDLED UP

THE TWINS

We are twin kittens.

There are two of us, and we look just alike.

Our brothers and sisters cannot tell us apart.

Even our mother cannot tell us apart.

When one of us says "Mew!" the other says "Mew!"

When one is hungry, the other is hungry.

When one is sleepy, the other is sleepy.

We are afraid, dear Queen, that we are beginning to be sleepy right now.

We have had such fun at your party!

TWO SLEEPY KITTENS

DO WE LOOK ALIKE?

We look alike and dress alike.
   And act alike, they say.
And that is why we're called the Twins
   By good old Granny Gray.

WHAT SHALL WE SING?

We are twins too, and they say we look alike.

We are so hungry just now, we simply cannot tell you a tale.

But we will sing you a song, if we can think of one.

Hey ding a ding, what shall we sing?

How many holes in a skimmer?

Four and twenty, we're feeling quite empty;

Dear Queen, give us some dinner.

Hey ding a ding, what shall we sing?

Dear Queen, give us some dinner.

WE'RE FEELING QUITE EMPTY

WAITING

We've washed our paws and noses red;
  We think we look quite neat;
We've donned our bibs, and now we beg
  For something good to eat.

DING, DONG, BELL

DING, DONG, BELL

We have something to tell!

All you kittens and cats who have told tales of rats, or of mice, or of cats, and have made our Queen laugh, listen!

The Queen bids you come to the grand dining room.

There a dinner she spreads

Which may quite turn your heads.

Heed what we say and we'll show you the way.

Ding, dong, bell!

THE DINING ROOM

Oh my! What a fine dining room, and how many tables there are!

Each cat has a table all to himself. I wonder why.

There is the Queen sitting at the end of the room.

She is looking straight at me.

Oh dear! What if I should spill my milk on this white cloth!

What would the Queen say to me!

I am almost afraid to drink it.

It is so hard to drink out of china cups.

But I must try.

QUEEN IS LOOKING STRAIGHT AT ME

I AM SO HUNGRY

I wish someone would hurry and bring me some milk.

Mine is all gone and so is my mouse.

I wonder if this is all we are going to have to eat.

I am so hungry I shall have to go home and catch a rat.

The Queen is asking someone to tell a story.

I believe she means me.

Yes, dear Queen, I will tell you a story about seven little pussy-cats who were not so polite as we are.

But first may I please have a little more milk to drink?

A HUNGRY CAT

THE QUEEN'S
TEA TABLE

The Queen has had the table set,
  As fine as fine can be,
And now I wish she'd send some milk
  For a hungry cat like me.

SEVEN LITTLE
PUSSY-CATS

Seven little pussy-cats, invited out
to tea, cried:
"Mother, let us go. Oh, do! for
good we'll surely be.
We'll wear our bibs and hold our
things
as you have shown us how:
Spoons in right paws, cups in left,
and make a pretty bow.
We'll always say, 'Yes, if you please,'
and 'Only half of that.'"
"Then go, my darling children," said
the happy Mother Cat.

The seven little pussy-cats went
out that night to tea.
Their heads were smooth and
glossy, their tails were swinging free;

They held their things as they had
learned, and tried to be polite;
With snowy bibs beneath their
chins, they were a pretty sight.
But, alas for manners beautiful, and
coats as soft as silk!

The moment that the little kits
were asked to take some milk,
They dropped their spoons, forgot
to bow, and—oh, what do you think?
They put their noses in the cups
and all began to drink!
Yes, every naughty little kit sent
up a meow for more,
Then knocked the teacup over, and
scampered through the door.

MANY THANKS

Sing, sing, what shall I sing?
Many thanks to my Queen,
    I will sing,
    I will sing.

Do, do, what shall I do?
    I will run away home,
    And go to bed too,
    And go to bed too.

I'M GOING HOME

GOOD NIGHT

Yes, I have put my jacket on,
  And my good night have said,
And now I'm going home again,
  And then straightaway to bed.

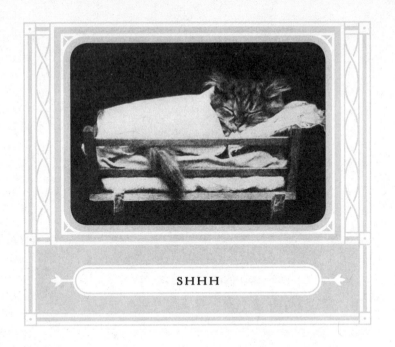

SHHH

THE LAST TALE

The book is done, the tales are told;
    Don't wake me with your noise.
For I'm as tired, as tired, I guess,
    As many girls and boys.

"Those of us who have
had glimpses of the child
heart and mind know
that stories of kittens and
queens and parties yield
much the same delight to
the little reader of juvenile
fiction, as do adventure
and romance to the
grown-up reader."

—*Eulalie Osgood Grover*

ABOUT THE AUTHOR

Eulalie Osgood Grover (1873–1958)
wrote more than 25 children's books,
including The Sunbonnet Babies books
and the Overall series. She was best
known for books like *Kittens and Cats*
(*Ye Olde Cat Memes*' original title)
that helped young children learn
and love to read.

ABOUT THE PHOTOGRAPHER

While the book, when originally published, was credited the Rotograph Co., it is more likely that **Harry Whittier Frees** (1879–1953) was the photographer. He is often referred to as the original LOLcat photographer, although he dressed and photographed puppies, bunnies, and other animals as well.

IT'S MY PARTY

CREATE YOUR OWN CAT MEME!

FILL IN THE CAPTION UNDER THE PHOTO
ON THE OPPOSITE PAGE AND WRITE YOUR
OWN CAT TALE BELOW.

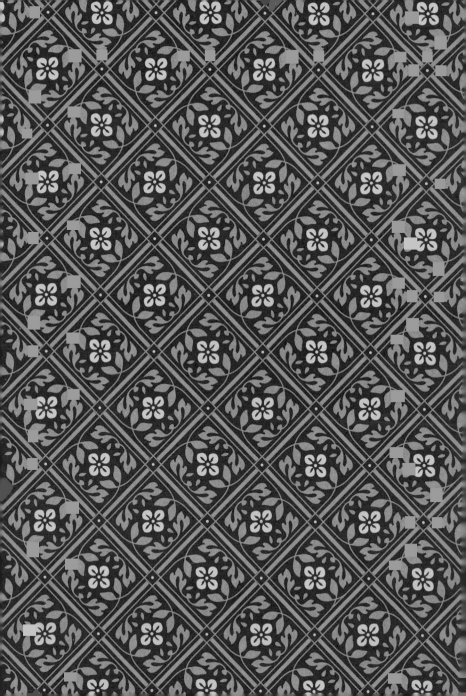